It is 2014.

It is 2014 and you are in Los Angeles. It is 2014 and you are in Los Angeles; you are 21. It is 2014 and you are in Los Angeles; you are 21 and confused. It is 2014 and you are in Los Angeles; you are 21 and confused, and you want to be loved. It is 2014 and you are in Los Angeles; you are 21 and confused, and you want to be loved more than you feel you deserve. It is 2014 and you are in Los Angeles; you are 21 and confused, and you want to be loved more than you feel you deserve but you think maybe you can hide it. It is 2014 and you are in Los Angeles; you are 21 and confused, and you want to be loved more than you feel you deserve but you think maybe you can hide it if you push all your feelings down.

It is 2014 and you are full of feelings.

First printing 2024
Published by Double Text Media
Long Beach, CA
www.doubletextmedia.com

ISBN: 979-8-9913662-9-8

recurring characters

Table of Contents

Incomplete Guide to Symbols and Metaphors

After Dave Eggers.

Cigarettes	=	Self-destruction
	=	Uninterrupted moments
	=	Breathing
	=	Expensive ways to kill time
Eggs	=	Vulnerability
Earring	=	Innocence
Kissing	=	Intimacy
Miles	=	Promise
Window	=	Window
Arms	=	Body
	=	Home
	=	Safety
Fuck	=	Destruction
Fuck	=	Intimacy
Fuck	=	Distraction
Fuck	=	Love
$10	=	Everything you have
Beds	=	Tenderness
	=	Seclusion
Breeze	=	A sign
Girl	=	Me
Poem	=	Me

Note: No symbolism is meant by the use of Denny's chain restaurants

Ephemera: I made you a playlist

for all the important moments you won't remember.

1. Aquarium - Nosaj Thing | Views/Octopus EP
2. Youth - Daughter | If You Leave
3. You Wouldn't like Me - Tegan and Sara | So Jealous
4. Some Boys - Death Cab for Cutie | Codes and Keys
5. Move You (SSSPII) - Anya Marina | Slow & Steady Seduction: Phase II
6. Ritual Union - Little Dragon | Ritual Union
7. Crooked Teeth - Death Cab for Cutie | Plans
8. Zen Brain - Nada Surf | High/Low
9. Devil Town - Bright Eyes | Noise Floor (Rarities: 1998-2005)
10. 3 Rounds and a Sound - Blind Pilot | 3 Rounds and a Sound
11. Sleep - Azure Ray | Azure Ray
12. My Silver Lining - First Aid Kit | Stay Gold
13. Take Me To The Riot - Stars | In Our Bedroom After The War
14. The Kids Don't Stand A Chance - Vampire Weekend | Vampire Weekend
15. Blue Jeans - Lana Del Rey | Born To Die - The Paradise Edition
16. Grass Stain - Waxahatchee | American Weekend
17. Hold On, Hold On - Neko Case | Fox Confessor Brings The Flood (Bonus Track Version)
18. Sorrow Sleeps - Rosie Tucker | Lowlight
19. For Blue Skies - Strays Don't Sleep | Strays Don't Sleep
20. Backwards/Forwards - Sarah Jaffe | Even Born Again

Playlist Blackout #1

Who I Saw First

The first time we speak
Miles is standing on the edge of the grass,
smoking a cigarette,
looking like the best kind of trouble.

This is not the first time I've looked at him
across an expanse of space,
but it is the first time I've seen him
looking back.

I don't know yet
that we won't go home together.
That I will think he is not interested
and he will think the same.

I don't know that months later,
he will sleep in my bed
and tell me we can't kiss.

I don't know yet that he will tell me
everything would have been different
if I had only chosen him.

He invites me to a party
and I don't know
that the window of opportunity
will slam shut on my fingers
while I am waiting for a breeze.

First Time

The first time I meet Jonathan
we are wearing the same shirt and
he gives me a fake name.
I give my phone number to a guy
who never calls.

The second time we meet, it is Halloween.
I am dressed as a Romani gypsy,
and trying to charm Carmen Sandiego.
He is wearing a sombrero and a kimono.
When I ask what he's supposed to be he says,
"Cultural appropriation."

The third time we meet,
he shows up late to dinner
and brings
stale cookies.
I am watching the shirt hem
of a guy I want to kiss.

The fourth time we meet,
Miles does not kiss me.
I am wearing my cute underwear
until Jonathan takes them off.

Sex Work

Jonathan says,
"With you,
sex never feels shameful."

I want to feel proud of this
like I coaxed something beautiful
from someone holding everything in.

But I can't help but wonder
if there are other things about me
that do make him feel shameful
and if maybe that's the reason
he only ever wants to have sex.

Jonathan says,
"You make me want to be
a better person."

I want to think this is flattering
that I have inspired something
in someone trying to find their way.

But I don't want to be wanted
for what someone else is not.
I want to be wanted
for my soft edges and broken parts
the slope of my neck, the curve of my arms.

I was not built to fill absences
any more than I was made
to be a space for men to fill.

Poem for Nice Boys Who Like Cool Girls

You've had your heart broken before
So you're not looking for a lot
But she sweeps you up in her whirlwind
Her flurry of hair and lips and too much wine

She makes you feel good about yourself
The sex is great
She loves your band
Says you're the nicest boy she's ever known

You love that she changes her hair
Every two weeks
Like she keeps time by her inconsistency
Getting tattoos to change her life on a whim

The idea of her is some far off thing
And she tastes sweet in your mouth
Burns warm against your skin
Pulling you closer, closer, closer

Maybe she's a little needy
Always asking for attention
You're not sure what's wrong with her
But you love the kinky shit she likes to do in bed

Most days she's bouncing off the wall
Or she's a puddle on the floor
Jokes that she's drowning in her daddy issues
And her lack of direction

She says she'll settle down
If you just give her some time
She'll stop kissing all your friends
She'll stop drinking so much wine

You're not sure when settling down
Became part of the conversation
This was always just supposed to be a weekend thing
Then a weeknights when you don't have other plans thing
A most nights if you feel like having sex thing

She starts calling you her boyfriend
And then texting when she cries
When you finally breakup with her
She tells you everything is fine

You're really glad to hear it
It's a relief she understands
Because you think she's really cool
And you really wanted to be friends

Close

I wasn't always there
When you were there
I was a million miles away
Or sometimes only feet
Outside, watching
Voyeur

Highly intellectualized
Not performative
Not more than usual, anyway
But goal oriented

I didn't take in rough edges against soft
Breath against skin
Every part of me against you
So busy thinking of how my body responded to you
That I couldn't feel my response to you

And now there is no you
Except the you I think of
The you with hands on my hips
My thighs
Biting and bruising in a watercolor across my chest

Pressing touching soft lips
Holding me holding me
Down down harder down
I'm right there I'm right there
You're with me and I'm right there
There there there
Only always there

And in my head
I come every time.

Note from 8209 Cactus Canyon Ct

When he asks what you are doing
what he really means is
Are you touching
yourself
Are you thinking
of him
touching you

So at least he's not
completely alone

Pearls before Swine

If a girl loses her pearl earring
in your bed
while you fuck her

give it back.

Even if you find it months later
after you have broken up
again and again and again

give it back.

Even if you are no longer speaking,
or touching
or walking her home in the dark

give it back.

Her mother gave it to her
and she meant to keep it safe,
keep it close–

didn't mean to give it away.

You'd rather not see her face
rather she be less than
a ghost–

want her to go away.

So:

Mail it to her house
where you've shown up drunk
so many times before.

Drop it in her drink
at that party where you will try so hard
to pretend she doesn't exist.

Hide it in the Marlboro Reds
that she brings every time
she knows she'll see your face.

She didn't mean to leave
anything with you.
Wishes that she never had

but
she didn't stop being human
just 'cause she crawled into your bed.

Pillow Talk

While I'm in bed with a boy that won't kiss me,
my roommate is fucking James Franco.
You think I'm kidding
but I'm not
he really won't kiss me.

We kissed as bodies but to kiss as people
that would be different
would taste and feel and hurt
different.

"And I don't want to hurt you,"
I say with my head on his chest
and his hands on the back of my neck
like spiders on the wall.

Later, in New York, Leighton Meister shows my roommate
photos of her wedding
while I hold his head in my lap and ask
to put him to bed
but beds are dangerous
for people like us.

Now she's on Broadway being quite the actress
and I'm on his mattress telling him,
"you drink so much
because you're sad."

Just like James Franco is sad
that he didn't fuck my roommate
one more time.

Note from 9830 Sierra Hwy

He asks what I do with these arms
when they're not holding him
Do they carry the weight of the world?
Do they carry the weight of your sorrow?

I wonder if he wonders
how many people have seen
the inside of these arms
or if all that matters to him
is the way that they hold him
close to my chest

These arms that ask him
to make a home inside of them
These arms that carve out space
for his body
These arms that have pushed away
as much love as they have taken in

What do these arms do
when there's no one inside of them?
What does this body do
when it is not a home?

I ask Jonathan's girlfriend what the beginning of a relationship feels like

She says:
Anxiety

She says:
Growing pains

She says:
Losing your balance

She says:
The air is saturated with them

She says:
It tastes, feels, smells different

She says:
A kind of jump start

She says:
It's too much

Ephemera: Text Messages #1

June 11. 9:53 PM

> Me: I wish you were here right now.
> I'm in a mood that no one else would get.

Miles: I'm flattered you feel that way.

> Me: I don't think I've ever felt a way
> that didn't feel like an okay thing to be around you.

Miles: That makes me really happy
and peaceful to hear.

Text Message Blackout #1

June 11. 9:53 PM

I wish you were
a mood no one else would

feel

June 11. 9:53 PM

I wish right now
no one else would

feel

happy

June 11. 9:53 PM

I wish you were

flattered

I've ever felt
around you.

The Porch, in five parts

I.

Miles asks if I torture myself with him
and I admit that I'm not sure.
He hopes I don't but
he doesn't want to tell me that.
He does tell me he would kiss me
if he didn't think that it would hurt.

II.

I tell Carter I'm not smoking any cigarettes
while the sun is up.
My line in the sand,
liable to wash away with the tide.
He lights up anyway
and passes it to me.

III.

My head is in P's lap
and I'm talking about how I think
I should marry a woman.
"You think that's the answer?"
P asks.
Maybe it is.

IV.

After his fourth Four Loko, Dave tells me
he's not ready to be in a relationship.
"I want to put my whole heart in," he says.
"But I'm selfish and immature and kind of a drunk."
I learn I'm not the only one who wants something
it's hurting them to have

V.
I ask Miles if we are dating-but-not.
He says we don't have the privilege
of being unobserved.
We could never have a clean break
with all the people
standing in between.

Poem I Will Not Write

everyone always thinks that
we're fucking
but we're not
fucking
how many times have i wondered
if other people aren't fucking
me
because they think
i'm fucking
you
sure
sometimes we smoke
each other's cigarettes
and drink
each other's booze
but a shared path
to self-destruction
is not the same
as a naked body
or the morning
on your breath
or the intimacy of
never quite trusting
but trying just the same

"Are you breathing just a little, and calling it a life?"

- Mary Oliver

We get blackout drunk
and wander down Vermont
hours disappearing into the night.

I wake up
zipped into my leather jacket
with a bruise on my face;
the only explanation for the pain in my neck
the shower curtain ripped from the rod.

When I am tempting fate
do I buy myself more time
by surviving to the morning?
Like playing chess with Death
but instead of an Ingmar Bergman film,
it's an episode of Jackass.

Is this what it's like to be living
or is the rushing in my ears
the sound
of a death march?

You can't tightrope a life line
across the valley of depression
anymore than you can float
at the bottom of a bottle.
But wouldn't it be something
if tonight we found we could?

Ephemera: Text Messages #2

June 14. 11 PM

Miles: For some reason I feel like I'm hiding something
from you though my mind tells me
I have no need to feel that way
Hard to talk my gut out of it though.
The long and short of it is i've been seeing someone out here.

Me: Ah.

Miles: I know I'm not obligated to tell you. But
maybe i like that you're open and didn't wanna feel
like I had a reason not to be

Me: I support openness.

Miles: I do too. Though I also feel like
I could have picked a better time to be open.
But it is what it is and it hit me now

Me: There's no good way
to say "I'm happy for you"

Miles: Haha maybe because when most people
say it they don't mean it

Me: You being happy
is a thing I think is good.

Miles: You're one person I wouldn't doubt
would mean it. I appreciate that.
Though I'd also say that romance is
a far cry from happiness, haha.

Me: It can help.

Miles: Would you ever tell me if you felt
I had something to apologize for?

            Me: Maybe.

Miles: Would you tell me now?

      Me: Are you actually asking me to tell
                you,
      or are you asking if in this moment
     I would be willing to tell you if there was?

Miles: I dunno
Both, I suppose

     Me: You weren't wrong about how the timing
       of your openness could have been better,
     but I don't feel like you should apologize for it.
   There's not anything I feel like you should apologize for.
  As for whether I would be willing to tell you (unprompted)
       if there was- I would like to think yes because
I tell you things, but right now I can also feel myself curling in
       and I'm not especially honest like that

            11:50 PM

Me: It's unlikely that I will ever feel like you should apologize
   for something. I don't really have that reaction to things.
   It doesn't seem fair to expect an apology from someone.

Text Message Blackout #2

June 14. 11 PM

I'm hiding something
from

my gut

I'm not
open and didn't wanna feel

openness.

But   hit me now

because

romance is

in this moment

11:50 PM

unlikely

Say the quiet parts loud

You ask if I really came
out here to walk you home.
Is the alternative

brush of fingers on
lips

hand on
open thighs

knees on
linoleum

knuckles against
sheets

You say you can't
give me what I want.
As if you didn't give me

sting of palm against
cheek

head against
shoulder blade

fingertip against
thin fabric

eyes on
bare skin

The $10 Poem

You pay $10 for parking
and you want to cry.

Stress builds like groundwater
and the nicotine and the desperate sex
are only poisoning the well.

You can lead a horse to water,
but you can't make it thirsty–
and you know he's not thirsty for you.
But is there a universe where he could be
or are you only writing poems for folks who don't want you?

Andrea Gibson says,
"sometimes the message in the bottle is 'don't drink so much.'"
But what happens when the bottle is
Zoloft;
Celexa;
tan pill;
pink pill.
Your favorite pill is Adderall–
generic is bright blue;
it's like coke except the doctor gives it to you.

Or in your case,
the friend you call Ratchet instead of Raquel
because she's drunk more than she's sober.
Once she tried to set you up with someone–

but you were already sleeping with him!
He broke your heart
but you still fucked him after,
and wrote poems for someone that didn't want you.

Months later—
a year from the time that you met
—when you egg his house
with free range organic brown eggs
he will know it was you from the sight of your car
the one you paid $10 to park
and that is a bitter pill to swallow.

Alternate Lives

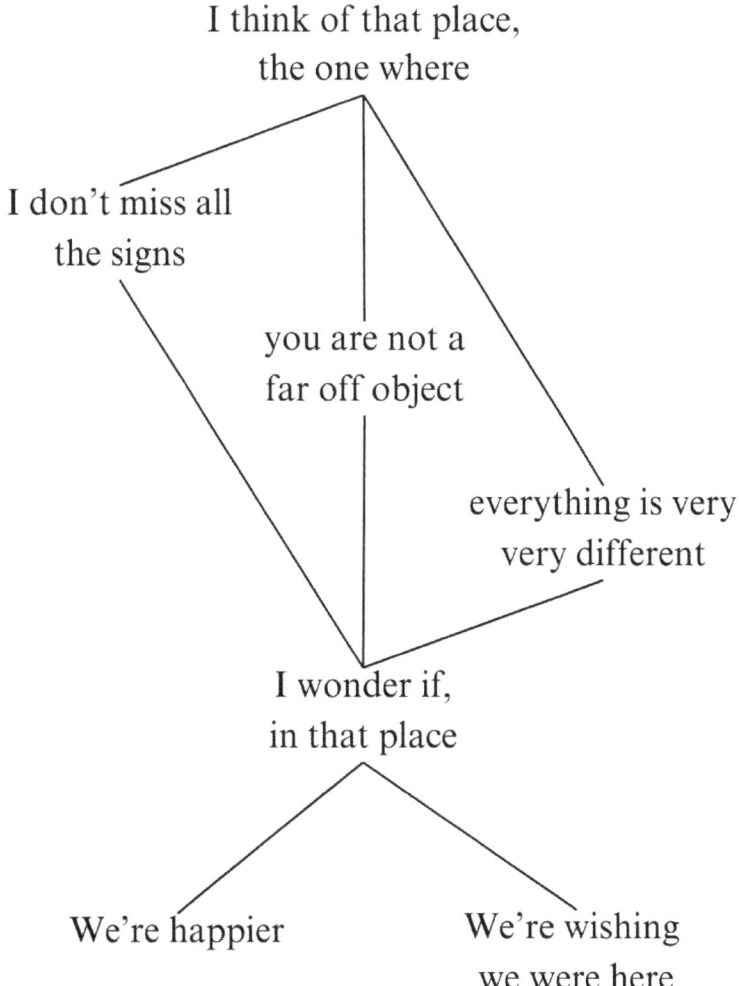

I think of that place,
the one where

I don't miss all
the signs

you are not a
far off object

everything is very
very different

I wonder if,
in that place

We're happier

We're wishing
we were here

And LAPD watches

While my friends are running drunk
through half-empty fountains
I am hugging Miles like my life depends on it.
This is often how we hug but tonight, especially,
I do not want to let go.

This is the snapshot
I want to hold in my mind.
Not the voice of the stranger who says,
"Listen to me,
you need to get your friend
help.
You need to get your friend some help,
or she's going to die."

I want to remember
standing in the night air
holding and being held

rather than hoisting Raquel
into the shower
to wash the vomit from her hair.

I ask Miles what the end of a relationship feels like

He says:
fuck

He says:
relationships echo each other

He says:
ends depend on who you discover the other person to be

He says:
you are messy and complicated

He says:
hold out hope you won't feel numb

He says:
maybe you can feel intensely again

Carter

You are six months sober and I want to ask you
do you remember when we sat in that dennys in downtown la
after they closed the one in the uv?
you were trying to write a novel and i was trying to write a
memoir but i didn't want to call it that.

i think that was the only time we hung out alone, unless you
count walking to and from parties.

we lived a whole life walking to and from parties.

once while walking to a party you asked me what it feels like to
be bisexual.
do you remember that?
i wrote a poem about it. and then i wrote an essay about the
poem.

the night i had to walk home so i could pick up my car
did i insist i didn't need you to keep me company,
or did i promise that i would give you half a bottle of wine if you
did?
you were drunk but i was sober,
or
mostly sober. i needed my car to pick up p's girlfriend, who was
too drunk to walk anywhere.
do you remember?

i kissed p's girlfriend. not that night, another night.
she was drunk then too but i was also drunk and didn't want to
think too hard about the way we passed her around.
i never kissed p but i wanted to.
i wrote a poem about that too.

you asked me if I egged your house on halloween.
i told you the truth instead of denying it.
i told you p encouraged me to do it.
you told me you had some girl in your bedroom and the sound of
the eggs against the house scared her.
do you remember?

there's nothing so satisfying as the sound of eggs cracking open
against the side of a house moments after they have left your
hand, two in each palm.
i wrote a poem about that too.

you asked if the eggs were just for jonathan or if they were for
you too, if they were for everyone.
i told you
mostly they were for him
but a little
they were for everyone.

on your birthday, before the eggs, you and miles walked me
home. from 29th street all the way to 37th place, practically
exposition.
i was shouting that i was the drunkest girl at the party
and you told me no, <u>you</u> were the drunkest girl at the party.
i told you not to placate me.
i told everyone not to placate me.

i woke up missing an earring, my keychain was broken, my jeans
were stained asphalt black and no one would speak to me. i
never wrote a poem about it.

do you remember?

Playlist Blackout #2

It is 2024.

It is 2024 and you are in Los Angeles. It is a different Los Angeles, and you are a different you. You are no longer living your life like a television show that may be canceled at any moment, pandering for views. But sometimes the reruns still air. Sometimes the old scripts feel like they were written just yesterday and those recurring characters are just off screen, waiting for their cue. You think, maybe, you finally know what the show was about, what the writers were trying to say. Or maybe not. Maybe it's only the familiarity of a story you have seen so many times before, the glow of nostalgia even if you didn't like the show the first time through. In the remake they recast you, and Los Angeles is really Toronto, but so much of the story is the same. They still fade to black at all the good parts, cutting away before anyone laughs or smiles or feels they are loved. There's no drama to be had from quiet kisses in the kitchen, or sunshine on the lawn. No series renewal for dancing in the living room, or sitting on the porch. But you know what ends up on the cutting room floor, what could only have ever made it as DVD bonus features. And maybe that's okay, maybe it is enough that you were there even when the cameras didn't roll.

It is 2024 and you are still full of feelings.

Annotations

It is 2014. (1) – The events of this book actually begin in 2013, but it makes a much nicer bookend to start in 2014 and end in 2024. Also when does any story really *begin*?

Incomplete Guide to Symbols and Metaphors (7) – After Dave Eggers' guide of the same name from his memoir, *A Heartbreaking Work of Staggering Genius.* Some people may also appreciate these sentiments from the final chapter: "You don't really care so much about the people who just get along and do fine, do you? Those people don't make it into the story, do they?" and "you cannot move real people around like this, twist their arms and legs, position them, dress them, make them talk–"

Ephemera: I made you a playlist (8) – Each song was released in or before 2014*. They were pulled primarily from elaborate playlists made for Miles, and Jonathan. Some played diegetically during significant moments, and the Author is grateful to the omniscient sound designer of life.
*The studio recording of "Sorrow Sleeps" by Rosie Tucker was released in 2015, however Tucker was playing shows in Los Angeles in 2014 and as such fits the somewhat arbitrary requirement that every song included accurately reflects the time.

Playlist Blackout #1 (9) – To the Author's knowledge, none of these songs played during an actual blackout, but given the nature of blackouts that might be incorrect.

Pillow Talk (19) – "beds are dangerous" alludes to many things, but the Author would like to note that it partly alludes to Miles physically falling out of his bed before the events of the fourth stanza.

Ephemera: Text Messages #1 (22) – The Author does not recommend keeping record of one's text messages for a decade, but it can have some practical uses.

The Porch, in five parts (24) – Dave also remarked, "I am Sixteen Lokos!"

Poem I Will Not Write (26) – In October 2014, the Author attended the Open Press literary festival. Someone read from a series of poems, which the Author recalls as being titled, "Poem I Will Not Write."* Thanks to archival research, the Author is 99% sure that the poet in question was Jane Gregory. However 1% of uncertainty remains because at the time the Author did not have a robust citation practice and simply thought, "oh shit I want to use that."
*Gregory's poems are, in fact, titled "Book I will not write" but 1% uncertainty, the fallibility of memory, etc.

"Are you breathing just a little, and calling it a life?" (27) – The title of this poem is borrowed from a line in Mary Oliver's poem, "Have You Ever Tried to Enter the Long Black Branches."

Ephemera: Text Messages #2 (28) – Some spelling errors have been corrected, but capitalization and punctuation (or lack thereof) have been maintained.

Say the quiet parts loud (32) – As mentioned later, there were many occasions of walking to and from parties. On one such occasion, the Author followed Miles outside with the intent of walking him home. Jonathan, having also been in attendance at this party, would go on to call Miles to express displeasure at this turn of events.

The $10 Poem (33) – The Andrea Gibson line quoted herein comes from the poem, "Glider Plane."

And LAPD watches (36) – The Fountain Run was a tradition at the University of Southern California, wherein seniors attempted to run through as many campus fountains as possible while wildly intoxicated. In 2015, it was officially banned by the university. The Author ran through not a single fountain.

Carter (38) – He is now several years sober, and the Author is very happy for him.

It is 2024. (41) – Those not familiar with the minutiae of on-location filming practices may need to be told that Toronto is frequently used as a stand-in for any major city, partly due to tax incentives for filming in Canada.

Annotations (42) – The Author invites you to ignore all of these annotations and make a blackout poem of your own.

Acknowledgments

Some thank you's are in order: to the Monday Night Writing Group–Christina, Nick, Kendall; to Ra for asking, "why not a book?" I'm not sure I would have done this had you not insisted; to the friends who read it, just because I asked: Angel, Joey, Ray.

All my love to the Word Buddies, who help me hold the space to write (with a special thanks to Lexxie for reading every version of this book and always asking for more). Slowly, but surely, we are filling up shelves.

I'm grateful to the mics who gave me the space to battle test many of these poems, and who will be hearing them for a long time to come. Without open mics, and the poets who make them special, this book would not exist.

Several of these poems have lived multiple lives, and I appreciate everyone who has been a part of their shape-shifting.

There are many people and stories that I would have liked to include but didn't. It turns out, I have more feelings than one book could capture and poems are an imperfect medium. Memories and people and hopes are too big for the page, but I'm still apologetic for everything that got cut at the bleed.

Christina, I know your name is on this page once already but I'm invoking you again to say thank you for reminding me that it's okay if what feels true now is different from what felt true then. I hope we keep making stuff together forever and ever.

If you made it this far, thank you too.